Howling Moon

Unleash your sanity

Poonam Sharma

BookLeaf Publishing

India | USA | UK

Made with ♥ on the BookLeaf Publishing Platform
www.bookleafpub.in
www.bookleafpub.com

Dedication

This poetic piece is dedicated to the person I have become pushed to grow in many senses.
These are the important phases and important people of my life. I am representing them through my words.

Thank you mummy and papa
Thank you Universe
Krishna Ji this is for you
My first listener of these poems " My Husband"

Preface

"Howling Moon: Unleash your sanity" is achieved through stories that build me more strong and complete. It is collection of emotions and self reflecting moments that you might relate to in many ways.
As you began to run through these poems I hope and wish you too will release what you feel inside connecting with your deepest fears, emotional rollercoasters and inner alignment with the universe. May you rediscover yourself all over again when hit rock bottom.

The purpose of this book is to accept what you were, what you are becoming and to observe if you are doing it all over again or making your own body or soul mourn. It's motive is to inspire the readers to talk not just about their happiest and glorified moments but also sad and harsh truths of life to lead a stable life with maturity and wisdom. The author will be utmost happy if readers can share your truth in times of despair and excitement with yourself first through journaling, sketching or any creative skill that one may possess.

Acknowledgements

Heartfelt gratitude to the universe who made me go through a beautiful spiritual journey that led me to my path and love for writing.
A valued thanks to all the hard and good times that made me reach this point.
It was a dream when these poems were buried in my laptop and the time has came when it will shine alive in real world.
Inspired from real life stories presenting to all my readers, your support and appreciation will be gladly valued and preserved.

1. P.S. She is my bestfriend

In the moment of darkness I will always shield your soul
to the moon and back
I would be the tint of orange glitch weaved in your spine
hovering at the zenith
Hiking through archipelago of those uncovered dreams
Providing you warmth of sleepsack when fireflies fly out
of sight
I will make the butterflies out of wasted kite

2. P.S. I still remember that night

The 90s moonchild was mortified by lurking toxicity
with connotation who's wrong or right
Maybe that's why "Mine" by Taylor swift became her
song on repeat for coming nights
The moonchild was not afraid of the snakes slowly
rolling up on the window as she looked effulgent in her
lavender essence on that valentine
Now she's in her thirties with husband named "Mine"

3. P.S. Unwrap 2020

Sun is dipping hard clouds rarely gather
All around in this month of May
To give surprise performance in band
I'm here in lockdown what else can I say
My wardrobe is disseminated like abandoned diamond or
particles of sand
Wait what day it is "Sunday"?
I looked in the golden watch tied on my hand
It's 1:50 PM already what a coincidence
I'm going to read "The Poetics of space" by Gaston
Bachelard
The End

4. P.S. Blinds are not blind but we are more

One pair of eyes makes you see what's rare

One pair of lips wakes up one soulful breath

One pair of heart is all it takes to create a pair

One pair of hands emancipate the soul

bonded with ego, misery, anger and despair

One pair of socks portrays immense care

One pair of leaves can flower a bud on earth

When it's time to address the birth

5. P.S. A Glimpse of Twin Flame

On 21st February 2021 walking through the winding
Serpentine roads of Shimla down the mall road
Featuring continuum of alluring cast iron and timber
Balustrade with monkey hopping here and there,
Catching your eye gazing at those cast iron and steel
Exposed colonial neo-gothic renaissance influenced
structures with steeply sloppy roof resting on pillared
porch, being an eye witness to restoration of what had
been burnt, enigmatic play of lights at night inhaling
cool breeze, feeling the sweetness of ice-cream after
having steamed spicy momos, feeling the warmth of
togetherness among the unknowns in the midst of
deodar forests, being an empathy to furry scared dogs. It
was enchanting love story where I found A touch of
eternity

6. P.S. Stop Getting Under My Skin

If you can't reply to my fragments of prose how can you
be my sentence. The insights kept nudging me to look
for gravity between the lines
You used to be my best listener once but now for you my
words has lost its shine
I am still the same benign soul
But our insane discussion is the main headline
In the building that's full of whine

7. P.S. I AM You

You see you while you do you little by little
When your consciousness renew to payback all that's
due
Simultaneously you witness repetitive numbers in every
preview
The greatest wealth is wisdom that's what they say gold
can only pay through
Consider you are one of the few in each step of this relay
Maybe that's what you inner soul somewhat always
knew
When the essence called spirituality hits you rock
bottom
Because your questions have been answered by the
symbols from the universe you pursue

8. P.S. 5 seconds from death

All blue wrapped in red on grey
Getting out of white with sombre
My eyes opened to single glance of my mother breaking
bad in tears eventually
Falling prey to maze of doors partially
With just one hand to hold time was crossing my mind
little harshly
Gazing through my eyes I was breathing slowly daily

9. P.S. He knew stories of my heart

I was on an unlisted journey to harshil
I took a big step of pursuing what I wanted
I was on a stop at crossroads with holding my deity close
to my heart
My and my deity identity was questioned which shook
me and closed me
The ever shining moon by the side of fire, water and
earth
Connected to me a soul who was pretty eager to witness
my wisdom and just what I have to say
Which made me think and see in reality this is what I
deserve
After that everything was just unexpected and non
imaginable

10. P.S. Late night with diagonal delight

Late twenties rolling towards left to align fanatically
with the round source instead of an agonizing rush
More than a curious eye it was a body lying diagonally
craving for that divine sight, but as the soul moved inch
by inch
the ecstatic vision on the board started slipping away
With extreme pressure tilted towards one side she asked
him
Could you please stay longer because i want to take a
good look at you?
Till my heart feel aligned with my soul chemically
Please don't go late twenties whispered. He was busy in
revolving
While she was a stable star at the centre of the whole
system ironically

11. P.S. I AM just an awakened soul

Just like the gatekeeper
Protecting the gate from dusk till dawn
The Gate shields thy inner soul, consciousness and
physical body
Similarly my awakened soul was grateful getting
through these days
For shielding my body while breathing cosmic energy
And my body reserved it for so long in other realm in
many ways

12. P.S. To all the spiritual being existing

You're not a creator
You're just a facilitator
Existing in this authentic universe to cater
Hope, Faith and Empathy
You are the narrator and not a traitor

13. P.S. A tribute to B&B

When everyone said get aside ew ew
She said hey come here enter the door
When everyone denied hearing her roar
He stepped in to be her onshore and offshore "Thor"
My parents burst into tears
when he passed away after 14 Years

She was like an uninvited 2 feet guest
with whiskers on her face leaving the house messed
She showed up at the east facing kitchen window each
day to ask for food at the same address
When lost in the dark she was rescued by a guard before
midnight
They made us learn the hard lesson the better way what
else to say animals teach us the right way but we are too
whiny to accept it anyway
They both were like the spiders on the web enclosing our
little hearts in many ways

14. P.S. It was a nightmare dressed like a daydream

I am ready to leave the battleground
But little do they know that I won't give up my cloak of
kindness just to be a part of that societal crowd
I am ready to leave my right for sitting on the so called
throne
But little do they know that I am not ready to leave my
kid's hands to guide them towards the best so soon
I can bow down a hundred times
But little do i knew that if you'll slam your own head on
concrete you'll only hurt yourself oftentimes
For love I can sow on a barren land with my injured
hand
But little do they know the same hands can voice if you'll
hunt on her island
I was ambushed from my own homeland I slowly
realised

15. P.S. My wedding vows pt.I

Dear future husband your body is a wonderland and I
want to be the flower that blooms everyday on it
I want to be the fresh essence adding to your personal
body mist
I want to be the sweetness that would always add
sweetener to your tongue
I want to be the raincoat embracing you in cold,
tempting, calm, chaotic rain showers
I want to be that woolen cardigan warming you up in all
seasons in the long run
Your sacred smile and gestures make my soul shine like
diamonds embedded in bright sun
I want to be the orbit in which you'll be the constant
always revolving

16. P.S. Polaroid Accessed By Five

Five kept developing the negatives under the shadow of
pink & white sky
Meanwhile treacherous snakes, aggravating rats, fallen
leaflets, empathetic pigeons,
howling wind, upside-down bats became her
overshadowing clouds passing by
She always said she will never marry someone like her
father then that could be some sort of parody
She used to say I will not be as suppressed as you mom
What she saw was becoming her reality
Everything was scary like a karma
woven in the fabric of her fractured heart
Yet she reclaimed her story like a phoenix rising from
ashes
To rebuild what is lost in between

17. P.S. Rented guitar with broken strings

Gazing through the window of my eyes
to sail the boat of my dreams past midnight
outreach the zenith of our amnesic storyline where
mountains and islands are having a tough debate that
who is going to host our memories not worthy more
than my stilettos painted in the pink sky

18. P.S. Untitled ringings

White essence wrapped in blue coat freezed in soil
Lying six feet under overburdened by the mockery
Chained onto the cross with the blood stains of flowers
Tied with gossip bells ringing in the turmoil
accompanied by three Letter word capturing their soul
for eternities

19. P.S. A life in a metro

It's not just a journey from start to end
It's not just women in one coach comprehending each
other
It's just a place to express emotions and energies.... The
mental rollercoaster they can never share with anyone...
A lady friend
Those women don't judge each other but are mere
empaths and just a nobody to somebody at the end
They laugh, they cry, they chant hare krishna, they sit
emotionless, they rant, they eat, they read, they fight,
they get sick, they sleep, they talk freely to blend
They are together by not being together to lend
The place I was running from became the safe haven

20. P.S. ILY Papa

It was cheerful merry go rides and evening treats that I
longed for the most in the land of ships
It was the morning bike ride behind your back which
still persists in my heart
Back in the city of tea gardens it was all the time papa
papa papa after coming back from school
In the greyish bloody shadows I expected the warmth of
your hand while waiting gazing at the door
My eyes always craved to get a glimpse of your face all
the time
My ears always craved to hear your voice whenever you
returned back from the office
I got ambitious,aggressive, rebellious just so we get more
talks
I kept looking for your face in the jungle full of wolves

21. P.S. A delightful stay in the hills

Just staying here was more than enough
Just hearing the sound of fresh flowing water was a
triumph
Just seeing the sun bloom each day passing by was solely
keeping alive my lungs
Just sitting in cafe listening to songs on loop made me
felt like "Bottoms up!
I wanted to go nowhere as it was more than somewhere
to have a clear laugh without rush
It was like a Disney World carved with forest like stuff
Decorated with curvy sloppy roads encircling the tall
mountains standing tough